MERRY CHR

Thank you so much for buying my book! Before starting your mazes journey, please read:

HOW TO PLAY?

1 Find the "Start" point on each maze and use your pencil or crayon to trace your way.

2 Carefully move through the maze without crossing the lines until you find the way through.

3 Make it to the "End" spot to complete the maze. Good luck, and have fun!

ENJOY THE SPECIAL GIFT INSIDE

https://bit.ly/*********

the gift in page 9

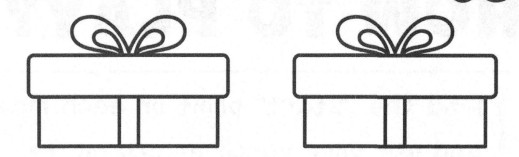

COPYRIGHT © 2025

CHRISTMAS

MAZE
BOOK

THIS BOOK
BELONGS TO: _____

CHRISTMAS MAZE : 01

CHRISTMAS MAZE : 02

CHRISTMAS MAZE : 03

CHRISTMAS MAZE : 04

CHRISTMAS MAZE : 05

HO-HO-HO!!

HERE IS YOUR GIFT
https://bit.ly/4eAC
VxP

Tap this link in the browser and enjoy!
if you loved the book and the idea
give us

CHRISTMAS MAZE : 06

CHRISTMAS MAZE : 07

CHRISTMAS MAZE : 08

CHRISTMAS MAZE : 09

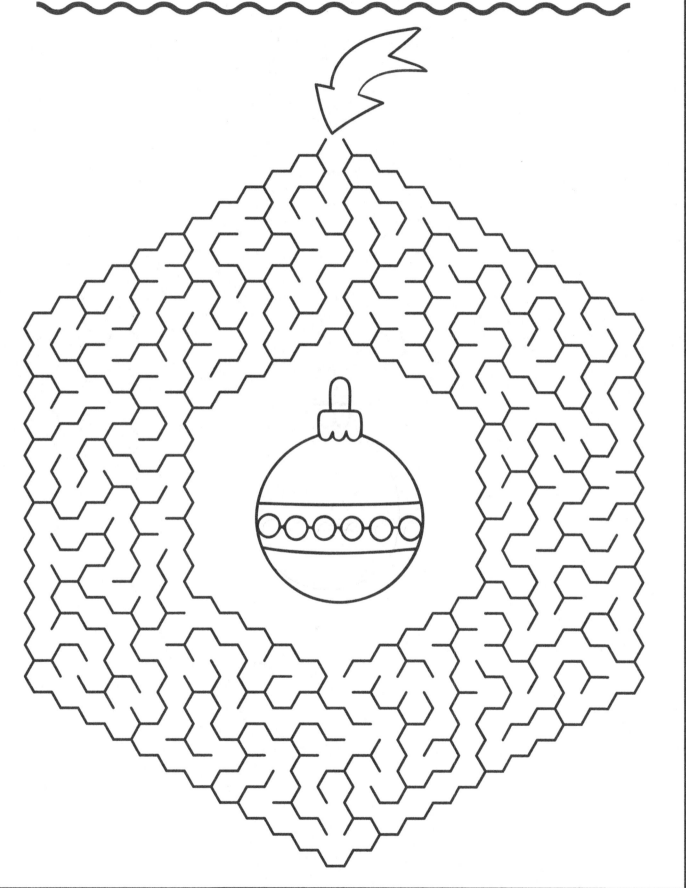

CHRISTMAS MAZE : 10

CHRISTMAS MAZE : 11

CHRISTMAS MAZE : 12

CHRISTMAS MAZE : 13

CHRISTMAS MAZE : 14

CHRISTMAS MAZE : 15

CHRISTMAS MAZE : 16

CHRISTMAS MAZE SOLUTION

Puzzle 1

Puzzle 2

Puzzle 3

Puzzle 4

CHRISTMAS MAZE SOLUTION

Puzzle 5

Puzzle 6

Puzzle 7

Puzzle 8

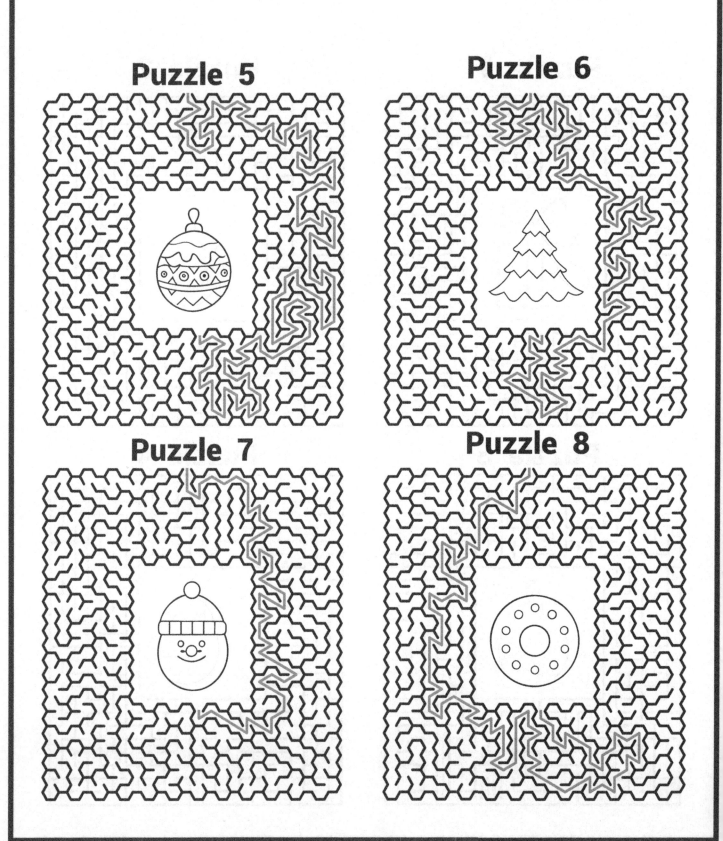

CHRISTMAS MAZE SOLUTION

Puzzle 9

Puzzle 10

Puzzle 11

Puzzle 12

CHRISTMAS MAZE SOLUTION

Puzzle 13

Puzzle 14

Puzzle 15

Puzzle 16

CHRISTMAS MAZE : 01

CHRISTMAS MAZE : 02

CHRISTMAS MAZE : 03

CHRISTMAS MAZE : 04

CHRISTMAS MAZE : 05

CHRISTMAS MAZE : 06

CHRISTMAS MAZE : 07

CHRISTMAS MAZE : 08

CHRISTMAS MAZE : 09

CHRISTMAS MAZE : 10

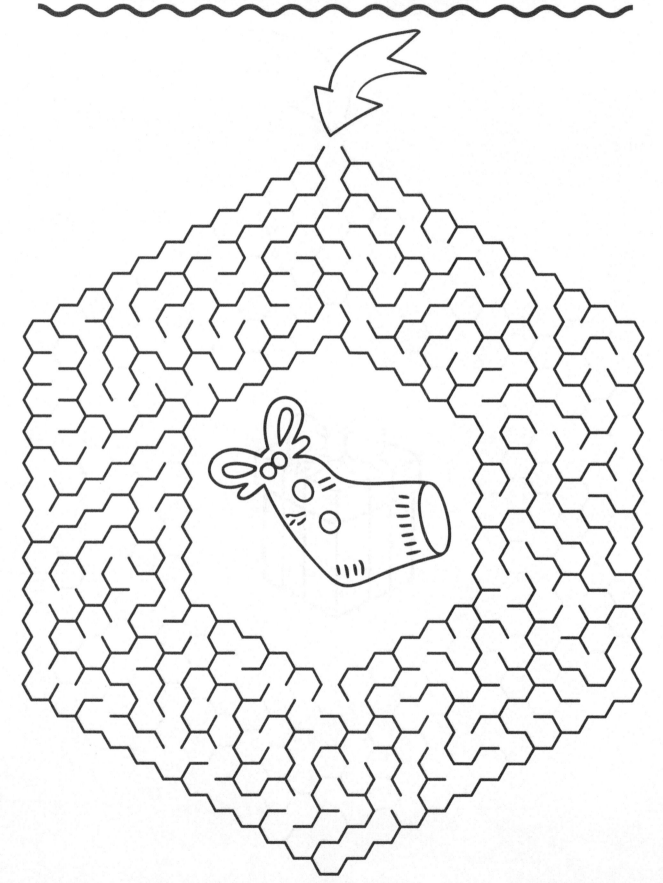

CHRISTMAS MAZE : 11

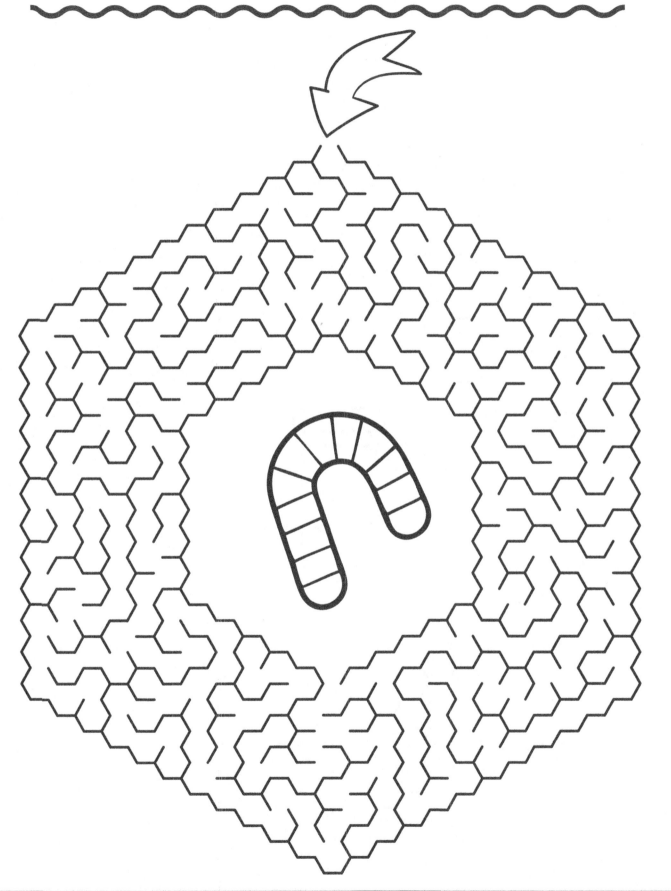

CHRISTMAS MAZE : 12

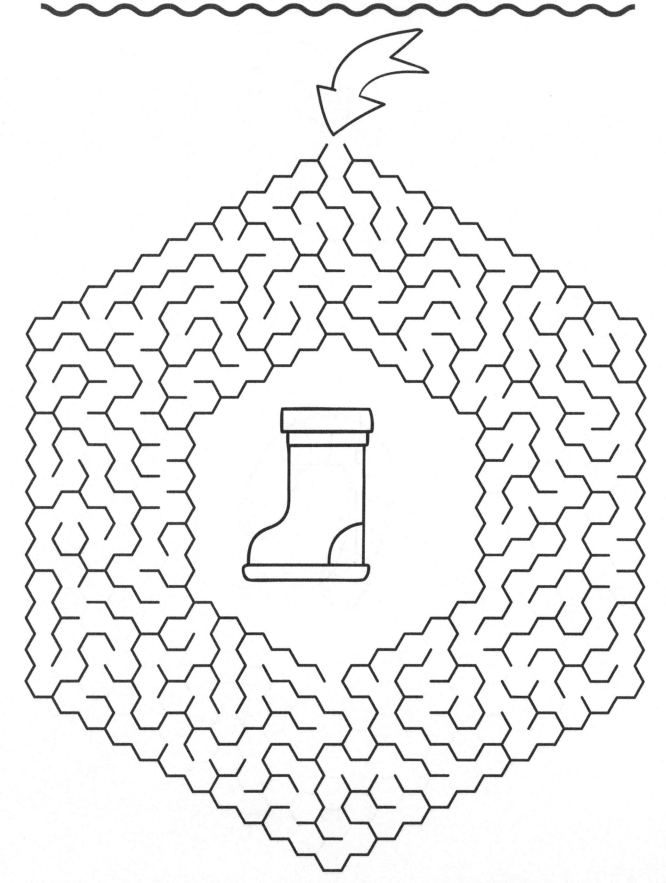

CHRISTMAS MAZE : 13

CHRISTMAS MAZE : 14

CHRISTMAS MAZE : 15

CHRISTMAS MAZE : 16

CHRISTMAS MAZE SOLUTION

Puzzle 1

Puzzle 2

Puzzle 3

Puzzle 4

CHRISTMAS MAZE SOLUTION

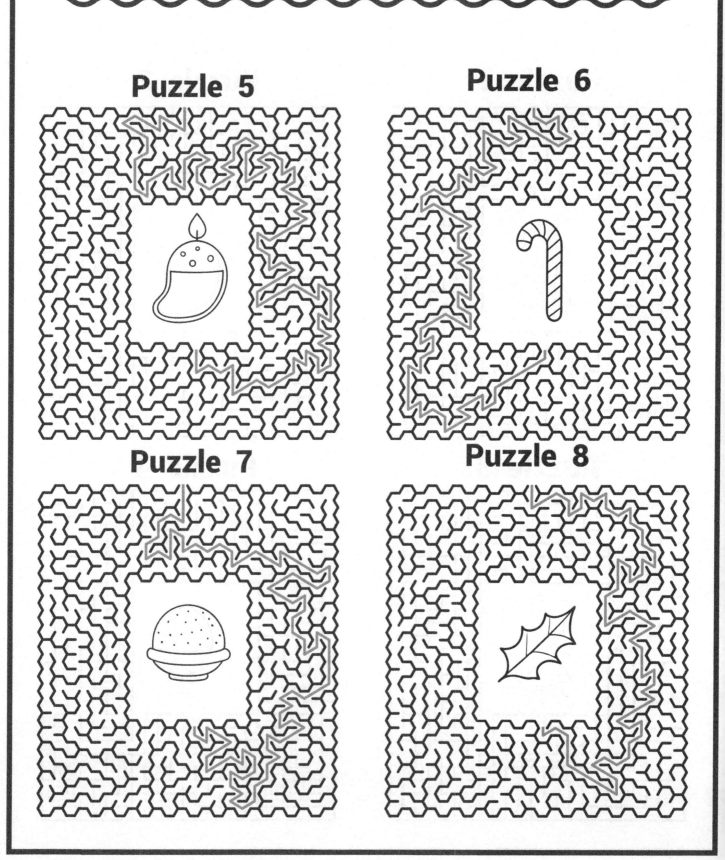

Puzzle 5

Puzzle 6

Puzzle 7

Puzzle 8

CHRISTMAS MAZE SOLUTION

Puzzle 9

Puzzle 10

Puzzle 11

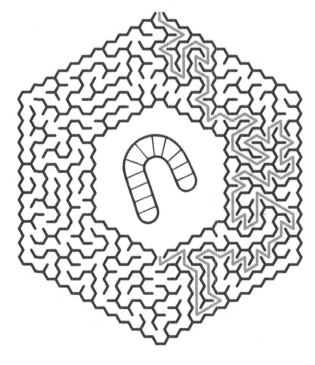

Puzzle 12

CHRISTMAS MAZE SOLUTION

Puzzle 13

Puzzle 14

Puzzle 15

Puzzle 16

CHRISTMAS MAZE : 01

CHRISTMAS MAZE : 02

CHRISTMAS MAZE : 03

CHRISTMAS MAZE : 04

CHRISTMAS MAZE : 05

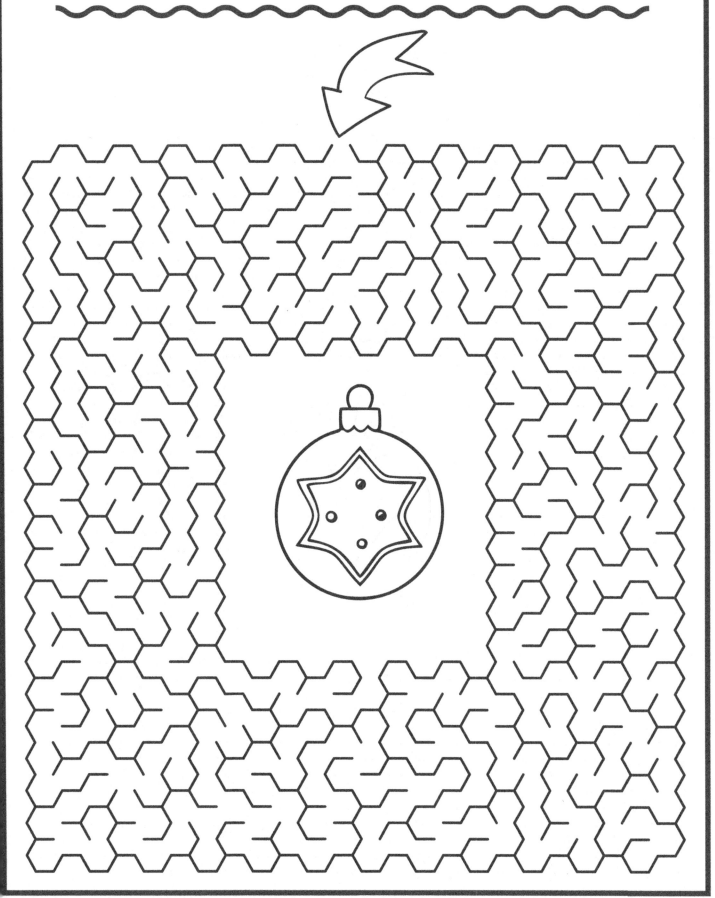

CHRISTMAS MAZE : 06

CHRISTMAS MAZE : 07

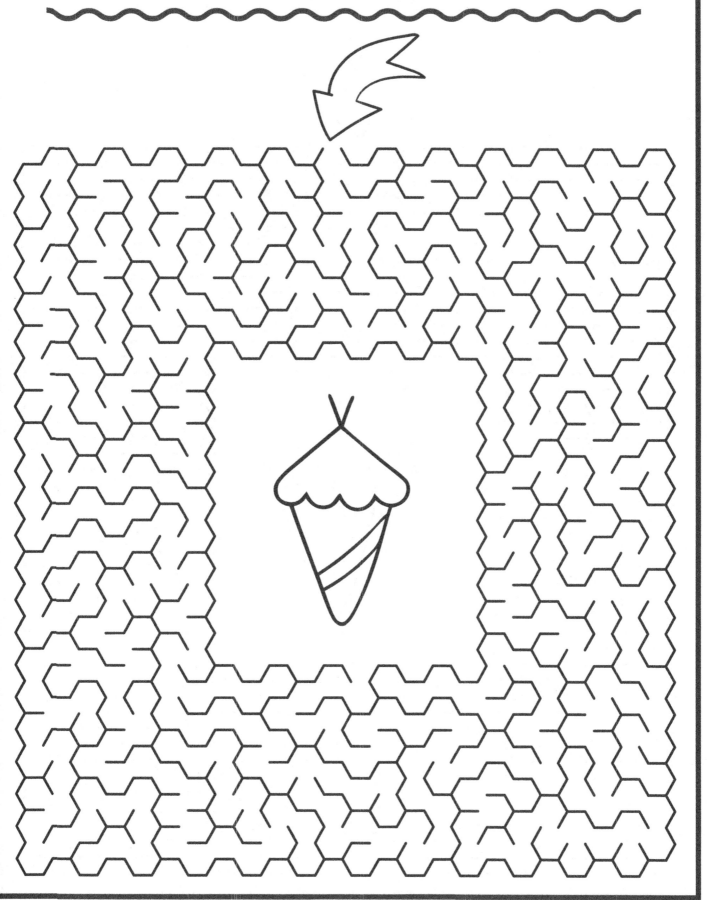

CHRISTMAS MAZE : 08

CHRISTMAS MAZE : 09

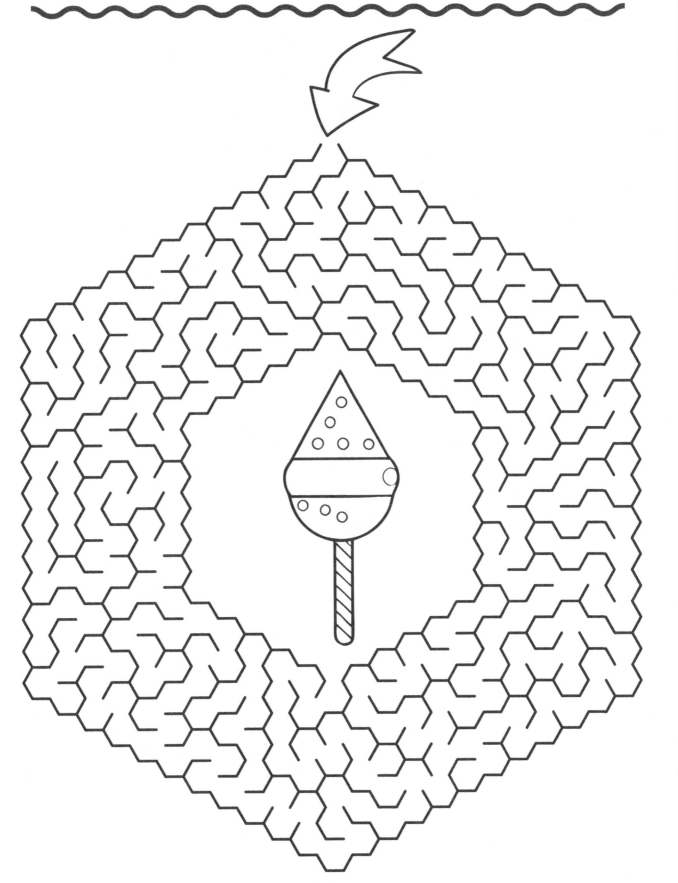

CHRISTMAS MAZE : 10

CHRISTMAS MAZE : 11

CHRISTMAS MAZE : 12

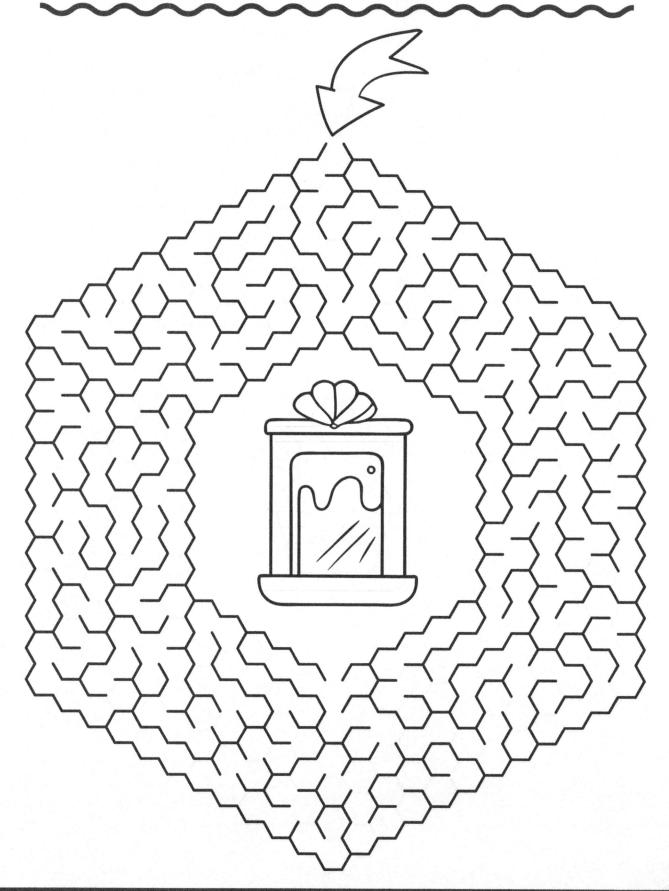

CHRISTMAS MAZE : 13

CHRISTMAS MAZE : 14

CHRISTMAS MAZE : 15

CHRISTMAS MAZE : 16

CHRISTMAS MAZE SOLUTION

Puzzle 1

Puzzle 2

Puzzle 3

Puzzle 4

CHRISTMAS MAZE SOLUTION

Puzzle 5

Puzzle 6

Puzzle 7

Puzzle 8

CHRISTMAS MAZE SOLUTION

Puzzle 9

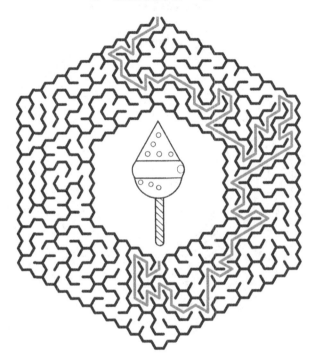

Puzzle 10

Puzzle 11

Puzzle 12

CHRISTMAS MAZE SOLUTION

Puzzle 13

Puzzle 14

Puzzle 15

Puzzle 16

CHRISTMAS MAZE : 01

CHRISTMAS MAZE : 02

CHRISTMAS MAZE : 03

CHRISTMAS MAZE : 04

CHRISTMAS MAZE : 05

CHRISTMAS MAZE : 06

CHRISTMAS MAZE : 07

CHRISTMAS MAZE : 08

CHRISTMAS MAZE : 09

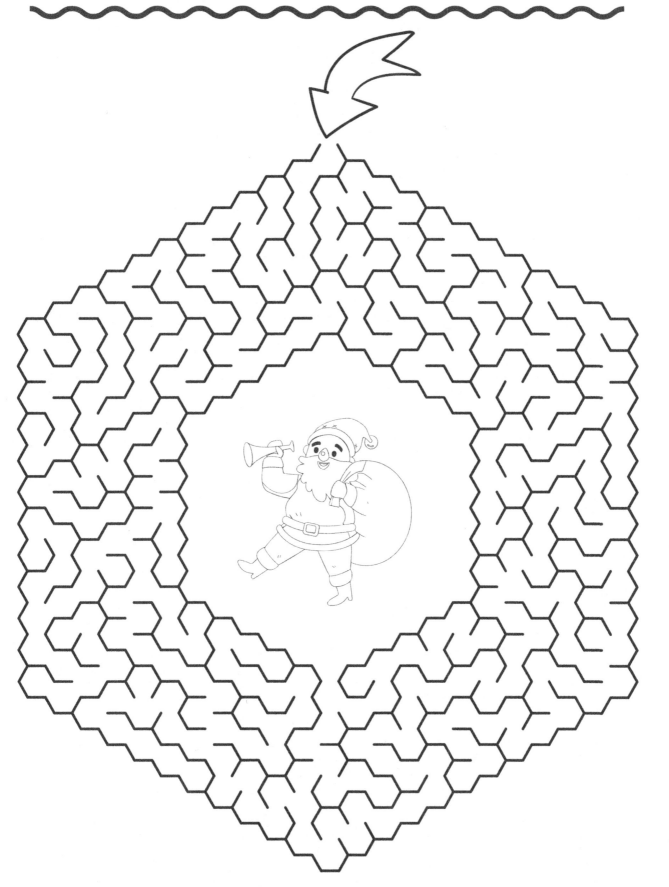

CHRISTMAS MAZE : 10

CHRISTMAS MAZE : 11

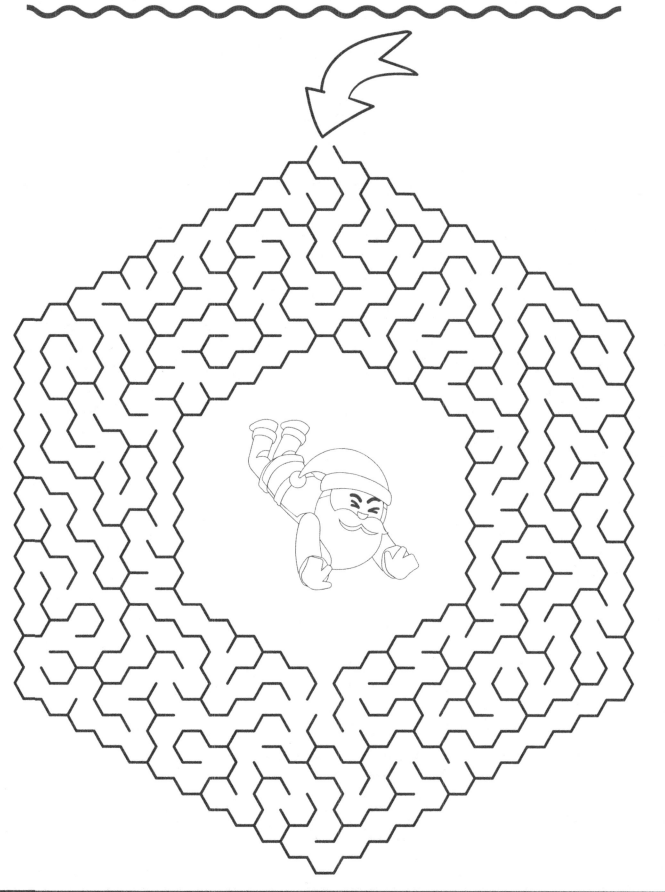

CHRISTMAS MAZE : 12

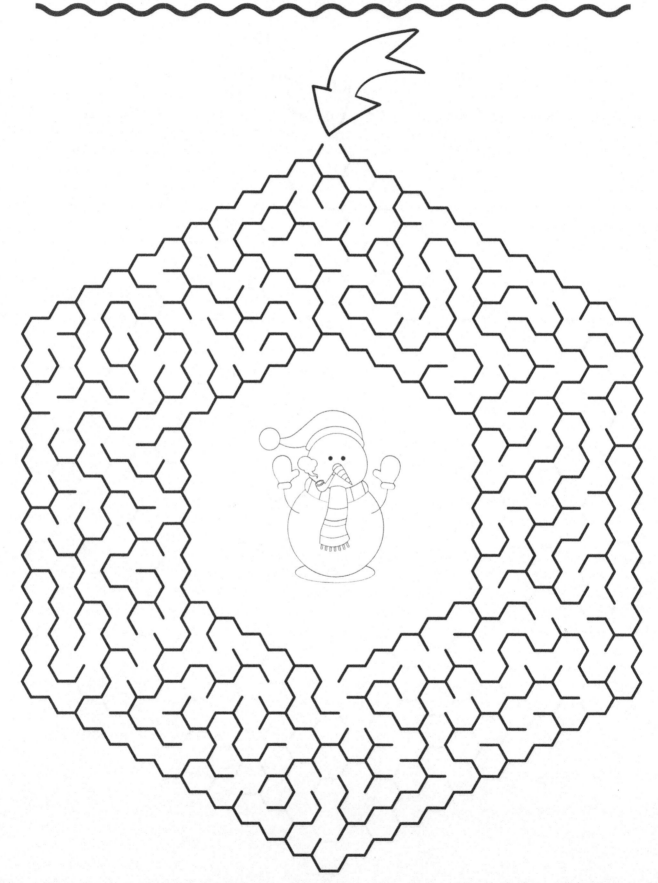

CHRISTMAS MAZE : 13

CHRISTMAS MAZE : 14

CHRISTMAS MAZE : 15

CHRISTMAS MAZE : 16

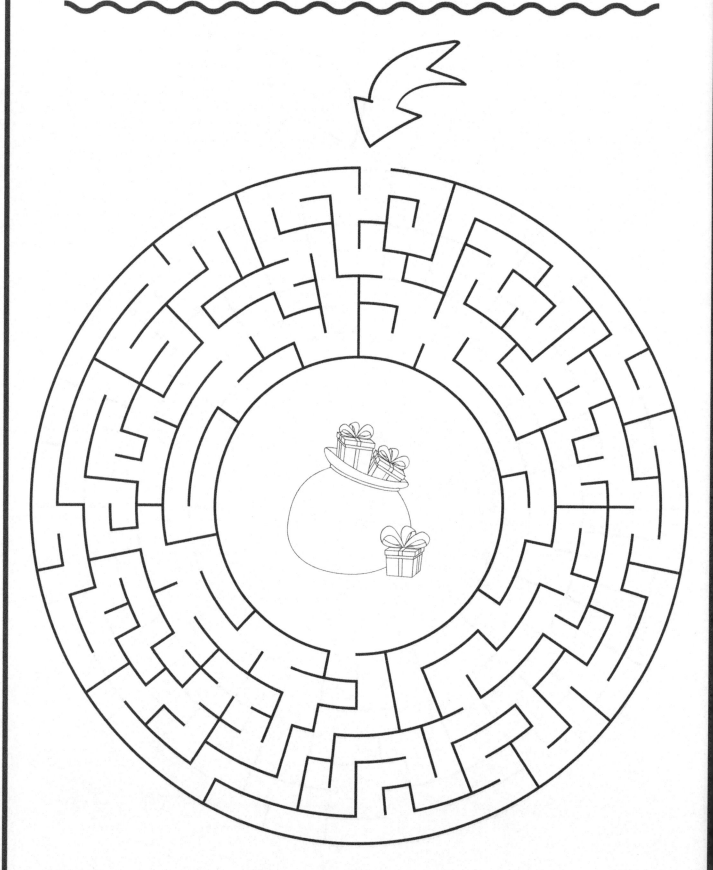

CHRISTMAS MAZE SOLUTION

Puzzle 1

Puzzle 2

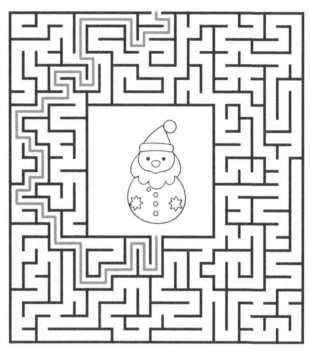

Puzzle 3

Puzzle 4

CHRISTMAS MAZE SOLUTION

Puzzle 5

Puzzle 6

Puzzle 7

Puzzle 8

CHRISTMAS MAZE SOLUTION

Puzzle 9

Puzzle 10

Puzzle 11

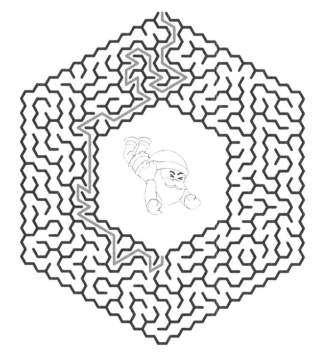

Puzzle 12

CHRISTMAS MAZE SOLUTION

Puzzle 13

Puzzle 14

Puzzle 15

Puzzle 16

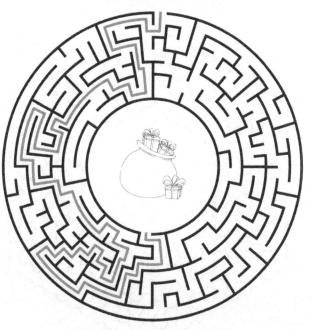

CHRISTMAS MAZE : 01

CHRISTMAS MAZE : 02

CHRISTMAS MAZE : 03

CHRISTMAS MAZE : 04

CHRISTMAS MAZE : 05

CHRISTMAS MAZE : 06

CHRISTMAS MAZE : 07

CHRISTMAS MAZE : 08

CHRISTMAS MAZE : 09

CHRISTMAS MAZE : 10

CHRISTMAS MAZE : 11

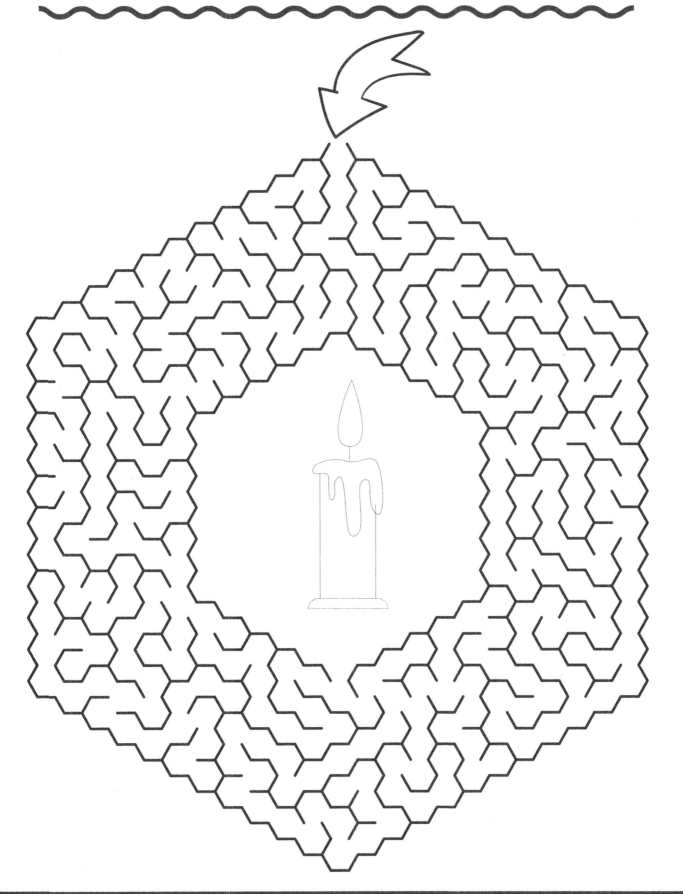

CHRISTMAS MAZE : 12

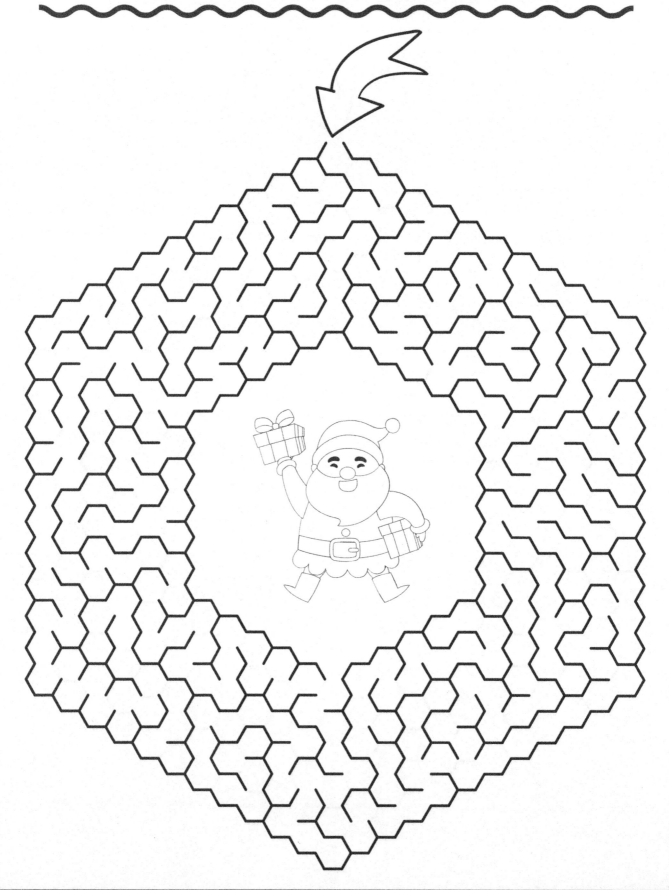

CHRISTMAS MAZE : 13

CHRISTMAS MAZE : 14

CHRISTMAS MAZE : 15

CHRISTMAS MAZE : 16

CHRISTMAS MAZE SOLUTION

Puzzle 1

Puzzle 2

Puzzle 3

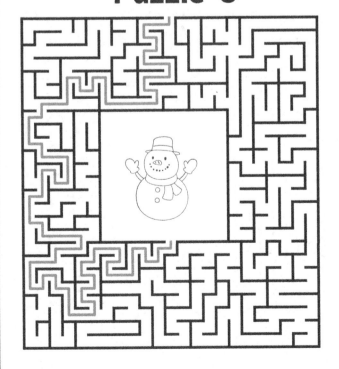

Puzzle 4

CHRISTMAS MAZE SOLUTION

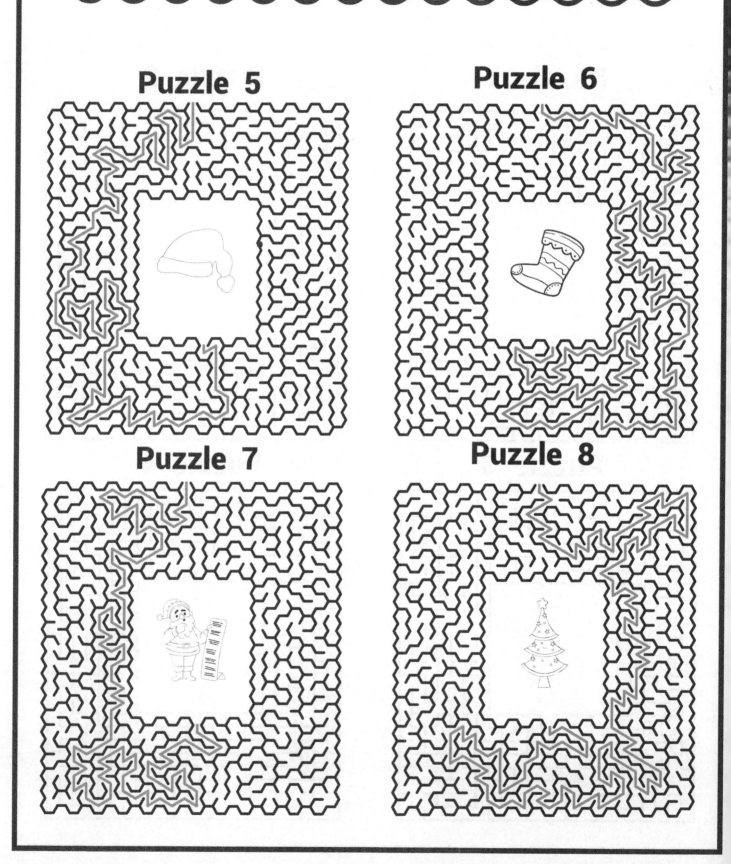

Puzzle 5

Puzzle 6

Puzzle 7

Puzzle 8

CHRISTMAS MAZE SOLUTION

Puzzle 9

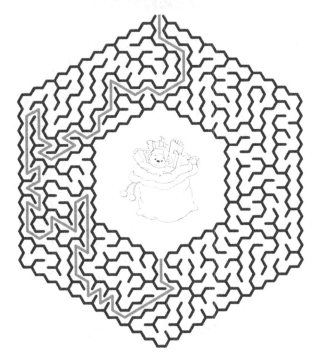

Puzzle 10

Puzzle 11

Puzzle 12

CHRISTMAS MAZE SOLUTION

Puzzle 13

Puzzle 14

Puzzle 15

Puzzle 16

Made in the USA
Las Vegas, NV
30 November 2024

12982075R00059